Open Doors for Preaching, Teaching, and Public Speaking

Derl G. Keefer

CSS Publishing Company, Inc., Lima, Ohio

OPEN DOORS FOR PREACHING, TEACHING, AND PUBLIC SPEAKING

Copyright © 2001 by
CSS Publishing Company, Inc.
Lima, Ohio

All rights reserved. No part of this publication may be reproduced in any manner whatsoever without the prior permission of the publisher, except in the case of brief quotations embodied in critical articles and reviews. Inquiries should be addressed to: Permissions, CSS Publishing Company, Inc., P.O. Box 4503, Lima, Ohio 45802-4503.

For more information about CSS Publishing Company resources, visit our website at www.csspub.com.

ISBN 0-7880-1876-0   PRINTED IN U.S.A.

*A special thank you for some men who have
encouraged me to write along my journey ...
Kenton Daugherty, Stan Toler,
C. Neil Strait, and David Felter.
Friends are forever and
I treasure your friendship! Thanks!*

Table Of Contents

Foreword by Stan Toler	7
Preface	7
Introduction	8
Index Of Open Door Topics	9
Open Doors: Illustrations, Quotes, And Quips	11
Mom Is More Than A 3-Letter Word	61
101 Tips For Holy Living In An Unholy World	67

Foreword

My good friend, Derl Keefer, through inspiring stories, anecdotes, and exciting illustrations, has created a "must" resource for every Christian leader. Derl is unparalleled in his ability to amplify the spiritual through stories! Someone has said, "Illustrations are windows of light." Certainly this book provides, with all due respect to former President George H. Bush, a thousand plus points of light! Each and every quote, story, and illustration pointedly deals with almost every subject under the sun! This book has the power to enrich the heart and to enlighten the mind. It will become a constant companion on my office desk. Enjoy!

Stan Toler

Preface

A door either prevents us from entering a place by being shut or allows us in by being open. This book is an open door to allow you to "come in" and enjoy what I hope are illuminating illustrations, sayings, and quotes to give practical help to your sermons and speeches.

I discovered early in my sermonic experience that people remembered the illustrations longer than the other material presented. A habit over the years of reading and collecting illustrations, quotations, and sayings developed into this book. I have rewritten the material, but I give credit to the original source and author. My desire is that you will be able to use many of these resources to illuminate your sermon, speech, or teaching material, giving greater clarity.

Keep opening the door for Jesus!

Introduction

Illustrations open doors to allow the light of God to enter your sermons. Every once in a while the minister finds the "perfect" illustration to glue his/her point together with his/her theological exposition.

The truth is that a single illustration does not make a sermon. David Buttrick describes a networking or "Image Grid" of illustrations that interact within the structure of any fine sermon.

Sermon illustrations must never distort the preparation of the sermon. When the body of the sermon has been formulated, the illustrations begin to give life to the thoughts.

The illustrations, quotes, and quips in this book have come from my files, books, personal experiences, and friends. I have given the sources when available. Although some of the sources have been lost over the years, the illustrations have remained dynamic.

Index Of Open Door Topics

Acceptance	11	Congress	22
Accountability	11	Country	22
Age	12	Creativity	22
Alcohol	12	Cross	23
Association	12	Death	23
Assurance	12	Decision	24
Attitude	13	Democracy	24
Beauty	13	Discipleship	24
Becoming	13	Ego	25
Bible	13	Encouragement	25
Blessing	13	Enthusiasm	25
Caution	14	Envy	25
Celebrate	14	Eternal	26
Change	14	Evangelism	26
Character — Christian	14	Example	26
Child	14	Excellence	26
Christ — The One Road	15	Excuses	27
Christians	15	Fairness	27
Christmas — Birthday	16	Faith	28
Christmas — Gift	16	Family Love	29
Christmas — Forgiveness	16	Fasting	29
Christmas — Image Of God	17	Fear	30
		Following God's Plan	31
Christmas — Room In The Heart	18	Forgiveness	31
		Friends	31
Christmas — The Star	18	Friendship	32
Christmas Wrapping	19	Giving	32
Church	19	Glory	33
Church Growth	21	God	34
Church Programming	21	God's Care	34
Commitment	21	God's People	35
Competition	21	Gossip	36
Conflict	22	Government	36

Grace	36	Revival	49
Gratitude	36	Ridicule	49
Happiness	37	Sacrifice	49
Holiness	37	Salvation	49
Holy Spirit	37	Satan	51
Homemaker	37	Self-control	51
Honesty	38	Service	52
Hope	38	Serving	52
Human Freedom	39	Smile	53
Involvement	39	Spiritual Irresponsibility	53
Jealousy	39	Spiritual Life	53
Joy	39	Stewardship	53
Laughter	40	Stress And Pain	53
Leadership	40	Stress — Good And Bad	54
Lie	41	Success	54
Life	41	Suffering	54
Love	41	Sympathy	55
Lust	41	Teamwork	55
Marriage	42	Thought	55
Money	42	Thoughts	55
Mortality	43	Training	55
Mother	44	Trials	55
Mother's Day	44	Triumph	56
Motivation	44	Unity	56
Nation	45	Unwanted	56
New Year	45	Virginity	56
Obedience	46	Vision	57
Parenthood	46	Word	59
Patience	46	Work	59
Peace	46	World	59
Persistence	46	Worship	59
Politics	46		
Prayer	47		
Pride	48		
Problems	48		
Progress	49		

Open Doors: Illustrations, Quotes, And Quips

Acceptance

Nothing devastates like rejection. It causes numbing despair and negative emotions. Richard Lee tells that G. Campbell Morgan, the famous preacher, wanted to enter the ministry.

"He gave a trial sermon in front of a panel of men who were to ordain him. To his amazement and despair, they turned him down for his ordination. Knowing his father was waiting for him at home in anticipation, Morgan sadly wired his father with one word: 'REJECTED.'

"He also wrote in his diary that day, 'Everything seems very dark. So still. But He knows the best.'

"Soon after, he received the reply from his father. It read: 'Rejected on earth, but accepted in heaven, Dad.' "

The memory of that deep, painful experience never left Morgan. Each person knows that type of pain. Be a positive influence on others by being accepting of them as Christ has accepted us. (Richard Lee, *Windows of Hope*, Sisters, Ore.: Multnomah, 1992, pp. 11-12.)

Accountability

Charles Swindoll relates that people who believe in accountability have four common qualities:

1. Vulnerability. This quality shows the capability of being wounded, shown to be wrong, even admitting it before being confronted.

2. Teachability. A deep willingness to understand, quick to hear and respond to reproof, open to be counseled.

3. Availability. This quality allows accessibility and touchableness, and even interruptions are viewed as important.

4. Honesty. The commitment to truth goes to the core of the spirit even if it hurts. There is a repudiation of phoniness or falsehood. (Charles Swindoll, *Living Above the Level of Mediocrity*, Waco: Word Books, 1987, p. 127.)

Age
"If we celebrate the years behind us, they become stepping stones of strength and joy for the years ahead." (Anonymous)

Alcohol
First the man takes a drink. Then the drink takes a drink. Then the drink takes the man. (Japanese Proverb)

Alcohol
"To put alcohol in the human brain is like putting sand in the bearing of an engine." (Thomas Edison)

Alcohol
Several years ago the *Bible Crusaders News* carried this thought: "Statistics show that 10,000 people are killed by liquor where only one is killed by a mad dog; yet, we shoot the dog and license the liquor. What sense is there to this?"

Association
When a dove begins to associate with crows, its feathers remain white, but its heart grows black. (German Proverb)

Assurance
Many years ago an older lady left her Buffalo home and sailed by boat to Cleveland, Ohio, to visit a daughter. A terrific storm arose, and the passengers feared they were doomed. They gathered to pray, but the older lady seemed quite unconcerned. She just sat praising the Lord. After the storm calmed, several of the passengers approached the woman to find out how she could be so serene in such terrible conditions. "Well, children," she replied, "it is like this. I had two daughters. One of them died and went home to be with Jesus in heaven; the other moved to Cleveland. When the storm hit, I wondered which one of my daughters I would visit first, the one in Cleveland or the one in heaven, and I was willing to see either one first." (Walter Knight, *Knight's Master Book of Illustrations*, Grand Rapids: Wm. Eerdmans Publishing Company, 1956, p. 14.)

Attitude

Howard Hendricks was on a flight during the summer of 1987 from Boston to Dallas that finally left the airport six hours late. Exhausted Friday afternoon businessmen fumed about the delay. Hendricks tells that the man across the aisle from him muttered under his breath every time the flight attendant passed by his seat. Hendricks contemplated talking with the guy, but realized the futility of such an attempt. Instead he walked back to the galley to compliment the stewardess on her self-control and the way she handled the circumstance. He asked her name, suggesting he wanted to write American Airlines and express appreciation for the way she balanced the situation. She responded, "I don't work for American Airlines. I work for Jesus Christ." (*Dynamic Illustrations*, Knoxville: Seven Worlds Corporation, July-August, 1996.)

Beauty

"The best and most beautiful things in the world cannot be seen or even touched. They must be felt with the heart." (*Friends Are Special Gifts*, Calendar by Daily Blessings, Inc., Bloomington, Minn.)

Becoming

"Nothing determines who we will become so much as those things we choose to ignore." (Sandor Minab)

Bible

"Many read the Bible like a butterfly, fluttering here, there, and everywhere; others read it like a bumblebee, digging for the honey." (David Wilkerson)

Blessing

"Buried under the biggest burden is a good place to find an even bigger blessing." (Janette Oke, quoted by Terri Gibbs, compiler, *Deeper Than Tears*, Dallas: Word Publishing, 1997, p. 34.)

Caution

"When you are in over your head, there is no better time to keep your mouth shut." (Michael Hodgin)

Celebrate

"If you're a believer — if you're 'in Christ' — then kick up your heels! Celebrate the Lord! Celebrate yourself! Discover a life of pleasure you never dreamed possible." (Anne Ortlund)

Change

Charles Swindoll, in his book, *The Bride*, writes that one of his mentors talked about his home church in the Midwest. One Sunday morning during an adult Sunday school class, someone introduced a new, trendy visual aid commonly used at that time in the business world called a "felt board." The poor guy was hauled before the church board and severely lectured. "How *dare* you contaminate our church with this worldly method!"

Change is never easy. Today's newest technology is tomorrow's antiquated method.

Character — Christian

Jill Briscoe expressed that she often heard her husband tell their teenagers that temptation was not just an opportunity to do the wrong thing, but was also an opportunity to do the right thing.

She writes, "Although we usually consider temptation in negative terms, God allows us to be tempted in order to provide us with a chance to be obedient. If we are to learn to say no, and we are certainly supposed to say no sometimes to some things, then circumstances become life's workshop to that end. Saying no when you want to say yes strengthens you, produces endurance, and builds character — Christian character." (*Time with God — The New Testament for Busy People*, Dallas: Word Bibles, 1991, p. 415.)

Child

"Fifty years from now it will not matter what kind of car you drove, what kind of house you lived in, how much you had in your bank account, or what your clothes looked like. But the world may be a little better because you were important in the life of a child." (Anonymous, quoted in *Chicken Soup for the Soul*.)

Christ — The One Road

Robert Shannan wrote of a religious congress for young people sponsored by the Roman Catholic Church on September 17, 1997, in Bologna, Italy. Two strong and unique personalities occupied the same platform that day. One was folk singer Bob Dylan who sang and played for the young people. The other was Pope John Paul II who desired to spend time with young people. When the Pontiff spoke to the crowd of 20,000 he referred to Dylan's classic song, "Blowin' in the Wind."

John Paul answered the song's title by expressing the thought that truly life's answer was blowing in the wind, the wind that is both the breath and life of the Holy Spirit. The Pope also answered the question of another Dylan verse that asked, "How many roads must a man walk down before he becomes a man?" John Paul stated strongly, "I answer you, One! There is only one road for a man and it is Jesus Christ who said, 'I am the life.' "

People of all ages are looking at different roads to salvation — materialism, New Age philosophy, Eastern religions, etc., but there is but one road — Christ! (Mike Duduit, editor, *Preaching Magazine*, Jackson, Tenn.: Preaching Resources, Inc., January-February, 1998, p. 48.)

Christians

"Christians are those who have shuddered at the awfulness of their sin because they have seen the holiness of their God. They have seen His justice in dealing with sin at Calvary. They are people who have repented of their sin and turned from it, because they have seen sin for what it is: willful rebellion against the rulership of God over their lives. And in turning from their sin, they have embraced God's only means of dealing with sin, which is the death and resurrection of His Son, the Lord Jesus Christ, on their behalf." (Kay Arthur, *His Imprint My Expression*, Eugene, Ore.: Harvest House Publishers, 1993, p. 61.)

Christmas — Birthday

Little Linda was allowed to pass out the Christmas gifts the Christmas Eve she learned to read. According to family custom, the one who distributed the presents would be allowed to open the first gift. After all the presents were distributed with care, Linda kept looking around the tree amongst the branches. Her father asked, "Honey, what are you looking for?"

The little girl replied, "I thought Christmas was Jesus' birthday and I was just wondering where His present is. I guess everyone forgot Him. Did they, Daddy?" (Eleanor Doan, compiler, *The Speaker's Sourcebook*, Grand Rapids: Zondervan Publishing House, 1960, p. 58.)

Christmas — Gift

Ann Landers tells that she had an attorney friend share with her about a special gift his father gave him one Christmas. The gift was a note that he wrote to his son. It read, "Son, this year I will give you 365 hours. An hour every day after dinner. We'll talk about whatever you want to talk about. We'll go wherever you want to go, play whatever you want to play. It will be your hour." That dad kept his promise and renewed it every year.

There are many children who would give anything to have that type of gift under the tree this year rather than toys or games. (King Duncan, *Lively Illustrations for Effective Preaching*, Knoxville: Seven Worlds Corporation, 1987, p. 87.)

Christmas — Forgiveness

An excellent devotional in the *Daylight Devotional Bible* states, "It was the perfect Christmas Eve ... the kind we all dream about. Dad was home early. After supper, he built a fire in the fireplace, while Mother made up a big tray of goodies. The kids jumped and ran and shouted in their excitement. Finally when their older sister arrived with her husband, the family gathered together in the den around the Christmas tree. They sang Christmas carols, exchanged gifts with one another, snacked on all the goodies ... then ended the evening by walking through the snow to the annual candlelight service. A Christmas Eve to remember!

"Christmas Eve. We plan for it and look forward to it ... A time of pleasant memories and nostalgia."

The author of the devotional then asks a poignant question, "Or is it?" He reminds us that for some families Christmas Eve turns out to be a great battlefield with mines and torpedoes mixed. There is no peace on earth, much less in the home! Our expectations often run high and our disappointments deep. The gift hoped for is the gift never given. The son who said he would be there — isn't. The sister who never has a kind word for anyone starts one of her many tirades.

"If that's your experience today, then even though it may be difficult, wrap up one more gift and give it away — the gift of forgiveness. It may be the most important, and most beautiful, gift you will ever give to another person." (*Daylight Devotional Bible*, Grand Rapids: Zondervan Corporation, 1988, p. 1263.)

Christmas — Image Of God

Guido Reni's famous fresco in Rospigliosi Palace in Rome, Italy, is called *The Aurora*. Like many paintings of the era it was painted on the ceiling of the palace! As you stand on the floor you have to look up to see it. Unfortunately, you can become dizzy and stiff-necked as the figures become indistinct and hazy. After several complaints the owner of the palace placed a broad mirror near the floor. The reflection of the picture becomes clearer, and you can sit for hours and contemplate the beauty of the work.

Frank Fairchild observed, "Jesus Christ does precisely that for us when we try to get some notion of God. He is the mirror of Deity. He is the express image of God's person. In Him God becomes visible and intelligible to us. We cannot by any amount of searching find God. The more we try, the more we are bewildered. Then Jesus Christ appears. He is God stooping down to our level, and He enables our feeble thoughts to get some real hold on God Himself."

That exactly explains why Jesus came at Christmas ... to show us God! (Walter Knight, *Knight's Master Book of New Illustrations*, Grand Rapids: Wm. Eerdmans Publishing Company, 1956, p. 78.)

Christmas — Room In The Heart

The boy was nine, but a big husky kid. The director of the church's annual Christmas pageant knew he would be the right one to play the innkeeper's part. With a harsh voice, his job would be to send Mary and Joseph away from the inn. He practiced his one and only line, "There is no room in the inn."

But the youngster had a flaw — his tender heart. As the night of the performance came he rehearsed his line again and again with his parents. Finally his turn came. With his gruffest voice he brushed the holy couple away from the door, saying, "There is no room in the inn!" Joseph looked so sad and Mary so helpless. They began to exit when suddenly the nine-year-old innkeeper blurted out to everyone's surprise, "Wait, come back here! You can have my room!"

The director thought the play was ruined! Some of the kids rolled their eyes. But the majority of people there that night at the local church thought it the best pageant ever. Many left with tears, recapturing the real meaning of Christmas.

Writing in the *Daylight Devotional Bible*, the author questioned, "This season is always so rushed, isn't it? And what suffers most? Shopping days? Parties? Gift exchanges? No, not usually. Time alone with God? That's often the first thing to go, right? No time, no room, for Jesus. Our lives are crowding Him out with too many things to do. Don't you see our Lord slowly drawing away from the door of your heart with downcast eyes?" "Wait, come back, I do have room for you." (*Daylight Devotional Bible*, Grand Rapids: Zondervan Corporation, 1988, p. 1084.)

Christmas — The Star

On Christmas Eve sometime during World War II, a little boy and his father were driving home from shopping at the grocery store in town. They drove past rows of houses with their Christmas trees and decorations lighting the windows. In several of the windows the boy noticed a star. He inquired of his father, "Daddy, why do some of the people have a star in the window?" His father said that the star meant that the family had a son in the war. As they passed the last house out of town on the way to their farm, there was a large open space. Suddenly the little boy caught sight of the evening star in the sky. "Look, Daddy, God must have a son in the war too! He's got a star in his window." He was so right. God has a son who went to war, but Jesus came into our world to go to war with sin, evil, and Satan. He has already come out the Victor! (James Hewett, compiler, *Illustrations Unlimited*, Wheaton: Tyndale House Publishers, 1988, p. 84.)

Christmas Wrapping

Frank Meade quotes from the First Baptist Church bulletin of Syracuse, New York, the following article. "There was a gift for each of us left under the tree of life 2,000 years ago by Him whose birthday we celebrate today. The gift was withheld from no man. Some have left the packages unclaimed. Some have accepted the gift and carry it around, but have failed to remove the wrappings and look inside to discover the hidden splendor. The packages are all alike: in each is a scroll on which is written, 'All that the Father hath is thine.' Take and live!" (Frank Meade, *12,000 Religious Quotations*, Grand Rapids: Baker Book House, 1989, p. 70.)

Church

"The church exists by mission, as fire exists by burning." (Emil Brunner)

Church

Fratricide, commonly known in lay terms as "friendly fire," is a military term used to describe one nation's accidental killing of its own troops. During the French and Indian War, George Washington reported that nearly four hundred of his troops were killed by "friendly fire." During the American Civil War, Confederate General Stonewall Jackson was shot by his own troops as he returned to his Southern lines. One military historian indicates that probably ten percent of the nearly one million American casualties of World War II — or one hundred thousand American troops — were the result of "friendly fire." The Vietnam War discovered that the percentage jumped to fifteen to twenty percent of the casualty list. During Operation Desert Storm, 35 of the 146 Americans were killed in the same manner.

How tragic, as the church fights evil, sin, Satan, and hell, to witness good lay leaders and pastor shepherds destroyed, not by the enemy's artillery, but from "friendly fire." (King Duncan, *Dynamic Illustrations*, Knoxville: Seven Worlds Corporation, January-February, 1996.)

Church

A young boy playing near an old, ornate church one afternoon decided to go inside. As he entered, he saw candles lit all around the building. He thought that it must be a great birthday party for Jesus, so he began singing "Happy Birthday" and going around blowing out the candles.

As the pastor entered the sanctuary, he noticed the candles were out and then caught sight of the young boy leaving. The minister thought, "It's about time that young man learned to have respect for God." Knowing where the boy lived, the clergyman decided to pay a little visit to his home and talk with his mother.

Arriving at the home, the pastor informed the boy's mother that he had come to discuss a serious matter with her son. The mother went upstairs, brought the child down to the pastor, and then returned upstairs. Left alone with the pastor, the boy looked at the minister.

The pastor asked, "Young man, where is God?" The question startled the boy. His eyes got big, but he said nothing. Again the pastor asked, "Where is God?" The question made the boy uneasy. His eyes got bigger, but still he said nothing. For the third time, the minister asked, "Tell me, where is God?"

With a scream the boy ran upstairs to his mother. Breathlessly he cried out, "Mommy, Mommy, they lost God at that church, and they think I took Him!"

Have you ever lost God? It's easy to do in this busy world of ours. We get our eyes off Him. In our religious activity we become so preoccupied with everything else that we lose sight of Him. Don't take a step without the knowledge that He is there! (Greg Laurie, *Everyday with Jesus*, Eugene, Ore.: Harvest House Publishers, 1993, pp. 33-34.)

Church Growth
While the whole world has been multiplying, we have been making additions to the church.

Church Programming
"Churches continue to offer the same old generic programming to a society that is segmented into a million different niches." (Rick Warren)

Commitment
"The greatest revolution in history would be if fifty percent of Americans who claim to have committed their lives to Christ would turn and begin to follow Jesus." (Dr. Paul A. Cedar, President, Evangelical Free Churches of America)

Commitment
In his excellent book, *The Good Life*, Max Anders tells that very few people in our world have never tasted a Coca-Cola. The one man responsible for that achievement is Robert Woodruff.

While Woodruff was president of the Coca-Cola Company from 1923-1955, he had a vision that he wanted everybody in the world to taste the "real thing" in his generation. During World War II he promised, "We will see that every man in uniform gets a bottle of Coca-Cola for five cents wherever he is and whatever it costs." Woodruff and his colleagues girdled the globe for Coke.

Anders comments, "Woodruff was more committed to giving each person in the world a drink of Coke than most of us are to giving each person in the world a drink of the water of life.

"As the church, our collective mandate is to take the gospel to the world. As individual members of the body, our mandate is to do what we can to contribute to that overall goal." (Max Anders, *The Good Life*, Dallas: Word Publishing, 1993, p. 68.)

Competition
"Anyone who believes that the competitive spirit in America is dead has never been in a supermarket when a cashier opens another line." (Ann Landers)

Conflict

Winston Churchill and Lady Astor met at Blenheim Palace, which was the ancestral Churchill family home. Lady Astor began expounding on a variety of subjects. She settled in on women's rights, an issue that was to advance her to the House of Commons as the first woman in Parliament. Churchill opposed her on this subject as well as many others that she held dear. Finally in exasperation, Lady Astor said, "Winston, if I were married to you, I'd put poison in your coffee." Churchill's classic response was, "And if you were my wife, I would drink it." (Max Anders, *The Good Life*, Dallas: Word Publishing, 1993, p. 189.)

Congress

"When Congress gets the Constitution all fixed up, they are going to start on the Ten Commandments — just as soon as they can find someone in Washington who has read them." (Will Rogers)

Country

"The energy, the faith, the devotion which we bring to this endeavor will light our country and all who serve it, and the glow from that fire can truly light the world." (John F. Kennedy)

Creativity

Florence Littauer relates the story that one day her daughter's teacher called her in to discuss why Marita had drawn a picture of Florence with purple hair. "The teacher, searching for some psychological truth, had told Marita to make my hair a 'normal color.' When I asked Marita why she had given me purple hair, she said simply, 'They didn't have any blonde crayons.' Marita's type of creativity wasn't acceptable to her teacher."

Florence goes on to say, "I meet many people who tell me sadly that they have no creativity (usually because their desire or creativity was wiped out by someone along the way) ... yet we all are born with a God-given ability to think creatively."

The God who created you uniquely has put inside you the creative juices to fulfill your one-of-a-kind destiny for the Kingdom! (Florence Littauer, *The Gift of Encouraging Words*, Dallas: Word Publishing, 1995, pp. 68-69.)

Cross

"If I were God and had to work out a plan for drawing humankind's attention from the basement of worries over food, shelter, and clothing, to the attic of faith and devotion, I think I would have chosen a different way than to hang my Champion-Son on a cosmopolitan tree.

"Admit it. Even all the excitement generated over the Easter news of the Resurrection cannot completely remove the barbs from our feelings about Christ dying on the cross. We happen to want our victories to be clear and concise."

We want to do all that is possible to avoid pain and suffering and especially to avoid the cross. However, we cannot avoid the cross if we want to be followers of Jesus ... can we? (*Preaching*, Louisville: Preaching Resources, Inc., Vol. IX, No. 5, March-April, 1994, p. 32.)

Cross

"The cross is rough, and it is deadly, but it is effective. It does not keep its victim hanging there forever. There comes a moment when its work is finished ... After that is resurrection, glory, and power, and the pain is forgotten for joy, that is the veil is taken away and we have entered in actual experience the Presence of the living God." (A. W. Tozer)

Cross

"Christ on the cross is the way Calvary really reads. For He died for us — in our place. We, then, are debtors. Strange, that so often we act like we owe nothing." (C. Neil Strait)

Death

"Take care of your life and the Lord will take care of your death." (George Whitefield)

Death

"Think of yourself, my friend, as a child of eternity. If the little ones around you are tomorrow's world, in a vaster, far more exciting sense you are eternity's world. You are part of the future population on the other side." (Anne Ortlund, *My Sacrifice His Fire*, Dallas: Word Publishing, 1993, p. 147.)

Death

"Someone has tampered with death — that someone is God!" (Bertha Munro, *Come Ye Apart*, Kansas City: Nazarene Publishing House, December-February, 1997-1998, p. 73.)

Decision

"The hardest decisions in life are deciding which bridges to cross and which to burn." (Laurie Baker, *The Speaker's Digest*, quote, February, 1994, p. 46.)

Decision

"Decision is the spark that ignites action. Until a decision is made, nothing happens." (Willard Peterson)

Democracy

"A democracy cannot exist as a permanent form of government. It can only exist until the voters discover they can vote themselves excessive gratuities from the public treasury. From that moment on, the majority always votes for the candidates promising the most benefits from the treasury, with the result that a democracy collapses over loose fiscal policy, always followed by a dictatorship." (Professor Alexander Tyler, quoted by Charles Swindoll, *Come Before Winter*, Portland, Ore.: Multnomah Press, 1985, p. 322.)

Discipleship

"The church is a community of disciples composed of all those who have believed on Jesus for salvation. In our day we have lost that perspective. Often people of the church feel as though discipleship is optional, that perhaps it is only for those who are extremely committed, or else it is for those who have been called to leadership or ministry. We must regain the perspective of Acts: To believe on Jesus draws a person into a community, a community that defines its expectations, responsibilities, and privileges in terms of discipleship." (Michael J. Wilkens, *Following the Master*, Grand Rapids: Zondervan Publishing House, 1992, p. 271.)

Discipleship

"Jesus personalizes the cost of discipleship according to what he knows are the priorities of a person's heart." (Michael J. Wilkins)

Ego

The *Dynamic Illustrations* Service told about a long-suffering wife who watched with interest one day as her egotistical husband stepped on a fortune-telling scale. He dropped a coin into the slot and out popped a card which read: "You are a born leader, with superior intelligence, quick wit, and charming — magnetic personality and attractive to the opposite sex."

"Read that!" the man said to her triumphantly. She did. Then she turned it over and said, "It has your weight wrong, too!"

Ego

"There is something magical that happens to the human spirit, a sense of calm that comes over you, when you cease needing all the attention directed toward yourself and instead allow others to have the glory." (Richard Carlson, *Don't Sweat the Small Stuff*)

Encouragement

"There is no better exercise for strengthening the heart than reaching down and lifting people up." (Lawrence B. Hicks)

Enthusiasm

"Most great men and women are not perfectly rounded in their personalities, but are instead people whose one driving enthusiasm is so great it makes their faults seem insignificant." (Charles A. Cerami)

Envy

"Everybody loves success, but they hate successful people." (John McEnroe)

Envy

"God even understands my shallow prayers that implore, 'If you can't make me thin, then make my friends look fat.' " (Erma Bombeck)

Eternal

Etched over the three doorways of the Cathedral of Milan are three inscriptions. Over one is carved a wreath of roses and written below are the words, "All that pleases is but for a moment."

Over the other is sculptured a cross, with the words, "All that troubles is but for a moment."

The great central entrance in the main aisle has this truth inscribed, "That only is important which is eternal." (Eleanor Doan, *The Speaker's Sourcebook*, Grand Rapids: Zondervan Publishing House, 1960, p. 96.)

Evangelism

"Not to share the gospel with Jewish people is like failing to tell a man who has a terminal illness that there is a permanent cure for his condition." (*Zion's Fire*, May-June, 1996, issue)

Evangelism

A young man approached Dwight L. Moody and stated, "Mr. Moody, I don't care for your witnessing plan."

Surprised, Moody responded, "Well, what plan do *you* use?"

"To tell you the truth," the young man replied, "I really haven't found a plan I like."

"Then," said Moody, "I like my plan better than your plan."

Example

"He who imitates evil always goes beyond the example that is set; he who imitates what is good always falls short." (Francesco Guicciardini)

Excellence

"The quality of a person's life is in direct proportion to their commitment to excellence regardless of their chosen field of endeavor." (Vince Lombardi)

Excuses

One young man told a friend that he did not wish to become a Christian. "Why not?" asked his friend. He replied, "Several years ago I was selling from door to door and was invited into a house to show my product to the wife and children. While I was demonstrating, the husband came home, swore at me, and kicked me out. He was a professing Christian. From that time I decided never to have anything to do with religion." His friend asked him, "Would you write down your reason in full and sign it?" With hesitation the young man did as asked. Then the paper was handed back to him with these words, "Keep this, and when you are asked for your excuse on the day of judgment, hand this to God." (Leslie Flynn, *Come Alive with Illustrations*, Grand Rapids: Baker Book House, 1990, p. 137.)

Fairness

An old French fairy tale tells about two sisters. One was bad, the other good. The evil sister was the favorite of her mom while the good sister was neglected.

One day at noon an old woman was at the village well needing a drink of water. The good sister also came to draw water from the well. The woman asked for a cup of water. The girl responded with kindness and gave the old woman a drink of cool, refreshing water. The woman, actually a fairy in disguise, was so pleased with the girl's kindness that she gave her an extraordinary gift.

"Each time you speak, a flower or jewel will come out of your mouth," said the woman.

The young girl was late getting home and her mother scolded her for her tardiness. She began to apologize profusely, and immediately two roses, two pearls, and two diamonds sprouted out of her mouth.

It amazed her mother. The girl told of her chance meeting with the old woman. The mother quickly called her other daughter and told her to go get the same gift. The bad daughter was extremely reluctant to be seen doing the humbling task of drawing water, so she griped and groaned all the way to the well.

As she approached the well a beautiful queenly woman — that same fairy in another disguise — came and asked for a drink. Blatantly disagreeable, the girl responded with a gruff manner. As a result, she, too, received a gift. Every time she opened her mouth, she emitted snakes and frogs. (Charles Swindoll, *Hope Again*, Dallas: Word Publishing, 1996, pp. 133-134.)

Faith

"Passage through the darkness of doubts and crisis ... is essential to growth in the process of faith." (John Powell, quoted by Terri Gibbs, compiler, *Deeper Than Tears*, Dallas: Word Publishing, 1997, p. 38.)

Faith

"Another person's testimony can encourage our faith, but only our own experience can empower it. As we consciously acknowledge Christ's leadership in our behavior, we sanction the talk of our walk." (Virgil Hurley)

Faith

Faith honors God; God honors faith.

Faith

"Doubt without faith is total defeat; faith without doubt is total victory." (Anonymous)

Faith

Faith is seeing light with your heart, when all your eyes see is the darkness ahead.

Faith

Dr. Tom Barnard wrote that he had heard the late Edward John Carnell define faith as "resting in the sufficiency of the evidences." Barnard stated that at the time he wasn't sure what Carnell meant. Dr. Barnard wrote, "Only much later, when I had lived a few more years and had seen God do things far beyond my ability to comprehend, could I understand Carnell's drift. 'Resting in the sufficiency of the evidences' means that God is at work, and He has left plenty of evidence around so that no human could take credit for it."

Family Love

Neil Kurshan tells a heart-wrenching story about a medical student who went to a counselor about whether she should complete medical school or drop out to raise a family. The counselor suggested that she could do both with a little outside help. The student related that she had promised herself never to entrust her children to a housekeeper. Wondering why, the counselor probed the young woman for an explanation.

"Well," the young student replied, "when I was a child, my parents would vacation in Europe each summer and leave me with a nanny. One spring, when I was eleven, our housekeeper up and quit suddenly. My parents were extremely upset that the vacation was jeopardized. Shortly before the departure date arrived they found another woman to take my regular nanny's place. I noticed Mom was wrapping up all the family silverware and jewels. Since it had never been done before I asked why. She explained to me that the new maid could not be trusted with the family valuables. I felt so hurt. Wasn't I a 'family valuable' of more worth than knives and forks? I never forgot the incident, and as I grew up I promised myself that I would bring up my own children without the help of any outsider."

Parents need to demonstrate to their children their love! (*Dynamic Preaching*, Knoxville: Seven Worlds Corporation, No. 1, January, 1995, p. 6.)

Fasting

"Eating is the granddaddy of all appetites. Fasting is a commitment to bring about self-control and overcome every other conceivable temptation." (Neil Anderson, quoted by Bill Bright, *The Coming Revival*, Orlando, Fla.: New Life Publications, 1995, p. 97.)

Fasting

Dr. Bill Bright writes, "Fasting reduces the power of self so that the Holy Spirit can do a more intense work within us." He offers seven biblical insights gleaned from the writings of the Scripture, Church Fathers, and Christian leaders of today.

1. It is a biblical way to humble oneself in the sight of a holy God (Psalm 35:13; Ezra 8:21).

2. It brings revelation by the Holy Spirit of a person's true spiritual condition. The result brings brokenness, repentance, and change.

3. It ushers in an avenue for personal revival because it brings the inner workings of the Holy Spirit into play in an unusual and powerful way.

4. The Word of God is more meaningful, vital, practical as we read and understand the Bible.

5. It literally transforms prayer into a richer and more personal experience.

6. It can result in dynamic personal revival — being controlled and led by the Spirit and regaining a strong sense of spiritual determination.

7. It can restore the loss of one's first love for our Lord. (Bill Bright, *The Coming Revival*, Orlando, Fla.: New Life Publications, 1995, pp. 92-93.)

Fear

Gus D'Amato, a renowned boxing trainer said, "Heroes and cowards feel exactly the same fear; heroes just react differently."

Fear

"Being free to fail means that we must overcome real fears — the fear of being criticized and judged, the fear of being inadequate for the job, the fear of overdoing the job and losing all enthusiasm." (Stan Toler, *The People Principle*, Kansas City: Beacon Hill Press of Kansas City, 1997, p. 34.)

Following God's Plan

A young woman felt compelled to go to India as a missionary. During her preparation to leave for her "new" country, her mother was in an accident. She delayed her trip in order to remain by her mother's side. Three years later her mother died. On her deathbed she requested that her daughter go out west and visit her sister.

The young woman did as she was requested. She was still planning on going to India, as soon as she had completed visiting with her sister. When she arrived she discovered her sister dying from consumption and without proper medical aid. So, as with her mother, she stayed with her sister until she, too, died.

Once again her determination was to head for India. But once again a family member's death prevented her from going. This time her sister's husband had died, and five small children remained as orphans. No one would take the five children. She determined that she would stay in the United States and raise the children so that they would not be separated.

Her plans of missionary service seemed over. She would never get to India. She took up her sister's lonely house as her mission station instead and raised her sister's children as if they were her own. It was not easy, but God gave her His strength and help.

Later God showed her why she wasn't to go to India. Because, instead of letting her go, God called three of the five children she had raised to go in her place. She had followed God's plan instead of her own, and a greater expansion of the gospel was accomplished by three instead of one. (*Dynamic Preaching*, Knoxville: Seven Worlds Corporation, Vol. 9, No. 8, August, 1994, p. 22.)

Forgiveness

When God forgives us, He casts our sins into the deepest sea. Then he puts up a sign: No Fishing Allowed. (*Come Ye Apart*)

Friends

"God evidently does not intend us all to be rich, or powerful, or great, but He does intend for all to be friends." (Emerson)

Friendship

"The greatest service one can perform is to be a friend to someone. Friendship is not only doing something for someone, but caring for someone, which is what every person needs." (C. Neil Strait, *From the Heart of a Friend, 101 Words from the Heart*, Fort Worth, Tex.: Brownlow Publishing Company, No. 86.)

Friendship

Friendships are like an oasis in the desert encouraging us to push onward.

Friendship

"I thank God far more for friends than for my daily bread — for friendship is the bread of the heart." (Mary Mitford, *Friends Are Special Gifts*, Calendar by Daily Blessings, Inc., Bloomington, Minn.)

Giving

"If you ask for a dollar, you must be willing to give a dollar. A leader must model giving." (Melvin Maxwell)

Giving

Richard Lee describes the life of George Muller of Bristol, England, as a genuine giver. During the 1800s, Muller had a great concern for the children of his community. Many of these young people were literally running the streets with nowhere to go. There were few schools for them to be taught the basic fundamentals of life and they were growing up as illiterate leeches on society. Muller felt God's leading to establish a day school and orphanage to meet their needs — and God supplied those needs abundantly!

As a result of prayer, nearly forty million English pounds were donated over his ministry of 63 years. That totals to more than one billion dollars in today's currency. But the truly amazing facts of the story reveal Muller's art of self-sacrifice in personal stewardship. Not only did he care for over 2,000 orphans in his five homes, he also provided day schooling for 121,000 students, distributed 300,000 Bibles, 1.5 million New Testaments, 111 million tracts, and supported several hundred missionaries around the world. His own personal giving throughout his lifetime amounted to over two million pounds. At his death his personal estate was valued at only the equivalent of $850, and half of that amount was in household effects and personal items.

It would have been easy for him to have developed into a "taker" in life, but Muller overcame the temptation and was one of the true givers of money, hope, life, and love. (Richard Lee, *Windows of Hope*, Sisters, Ore.: Multnomah, 1992, pp. 42-43.)

Giving

"Those who give most are least concerned about returns." (*The Lunn Log*)

Giving

A government income tax inspector once visited a minister and asked to see his church. The pastor beamed with pride and pleasure at the request. The minister showed him the sanctuary, fellowship hall, the office complex, and anything else the tax man asked to see. The clergyman anxiously asked what he thought of the church.

"Well, to tell you the truth, I'm a bit disappointed," the tax man replied. "After looking at the income tax returns of your parishioners and the amounts they claimed to have given, I had come to the conclusion that the aisles must be paved with gold." (Eleanor Doan, *The Speaker's Sourcebook*, Grand Rapids: Zondervan Publishing House, 1975, p. 110.)

Glory

Joni Eareckson Tada mentions that she has learned what God is all about. His character or attributes — holiness, love, compassion, justice, truth, and mercy — are His glory!

Then she asks, "So how is it that you and I can glorify God?" She tells that every day we live we reveal His attributes. "Every time you share the good news of Christ with another. Every time you reflect patience in the middle of an upsetting or perplexing problem. Every time you smile from the heart or offer an encouraging word. Whenever those around you see God's character displayed in your attitudes and responses, you are displaying His glory."

Let's remember that God's glory isn't reserved for a temple of stone, brick, or mortar. Nor is it some heavenly panorama. "It can shine out clearly while you're changing a flat on the freeway ... or counseling an angry co-worker ... or lying in a hospital bed ... or balancing two crying babies in the church nursery."

God's glory is you! (*Time with God, New Century Version*, Dallas: Word Bibles, 1991, p. 435.)

God

"The world comes to know God when they see God's nature expressed through His activity. When God starts to work, He accomplishes something that only He can do. When God does that, both God's people and the world come to know Him in ways they have never known Him before. That is why God gives God-sized assignments to His people." (Henry Blackaby and Claude King, *Experiencing God*, Nashville: Broadman & Holman Publishers, 1994, pp. 140-141.)

God

"One-time baseball great Joe Garagiola stepped up to the plate when his turn to bat came. Before assuming his stance, however, fervent Roman Catholic Joe took his bat and made the sign of the cross in the dirt in front of home plate. Catcher Yogi Berra, also a devout Catholic, walked out and erased Garagiola's cross. Turning to the astonished Garagiola, Berra smiled and said, 'Let's let God watch this inning.'" (King Duncan, *Mule Eggs and Topknots*, Knoxville: Seven Worlds Corporation, 1991, p. 148.)

God's Care

Fred Musser was about to leave to study for the ministry when his pastor, Rev. Temple, stopped by and talked about God.

Pastor Temple said, "When my son was little, we often walked together out through the fields and neighboring pasture behind the parsonage. At first the boy would hold onto my little finger, but he found that when he stepped into a hoof print or stumbled over something, his grip would fail and he'd fall down. Not giving it much thought, my mind on other matters, I'd stop and he'd get up, brush himself off, and then grab hold of my little finger again. Each time it would be harder.

"It happened again. The boy looked up at me and said, 'Daddy, I think if you would hold my hand, I wouldn't fall.' "

Musser said that as Pastor Temple told him the story he did so with a tear in his eye. Temple said, "You know, he still stumbled many times after that, but he never hit the ground. Now, as you walk with God, don't try to hold onto Him, let Him hold onto you. You may stumble but He'll never let you fall." (James Hewett, compiler, *Illustrations Unlimited*, Wheaton: Tyndale House, 1988, p. 244.)

God's People

Lewis Timberlake told this illustration in a *Reader's Digest* issue several years ago.

While touring California he visited the area of the giant sequoia trees. The Forest Ranger guide told the group that the sequoia tree roots are barely below the surface of the ground.

Timberlake responded to the guide, "That's impossible. I'm a country boy, and I know that if the roots don't grow deep into the earth, strong winds will blow the trees over."

The Forest Ranger said, "That's true of most trees, but not the sequoias. They grow only in groves and their roots are intertwined under the surface of the earth. So, when the winds come, they hold each other up."

How much so it must be for God's people during the wind of adversity! ("Points to Ponder," *Reader's Digest*, May, 1989, excerpted from *Timberlake Monthly*.)

Gossip
"Most of us can keep a secret. It's the people we tell it to that can't." (Anonymous, quoted in *From the Heart of a Friend, 101 Words From the Heart*, Fort Worth, Tex.: Brownlow Publishing Co., No. 6.)

Gossip
Four ministers met for a social time together. During a lag in the conversation one of the preachers stated, "Our people come to us and pour out their hearts, confess certain sins and spiritual needs. Let's do the same tonight. After all, confession is good for the soul." After a while all four agreed. One confessed he liked to sneak out and go to the movies when away from the church. The second confessed to liking to smoke cigars, and the third confessed to playing the lottery. When it came time for the fourth to confess, he became reluctant. After much prodding from the other three he confessed, "My secret sin is gossiping and I can hardly wait to get out of here!"

Gossip
It is well to remember that mansions in the sky cannot be built out of the mud thrown at others! (*Evangelist* magazine)

Government
"The care of human life and happiness, and not their destruction, is the first and only legitimate object of good government." (Thomas Jefferson)

Grace
"Our minds must be fixed upon grace, otherwise we will always be overwhelmed and withdrawn from the Presence of God." (Francis Fragipane, *Holiness, Truth, and the Presence of God*)

Gratitude
"If you pick up a starving dog and make him prosperous, he will not bite you. That is the principle difference between a dog and a man." (Mark Twain)

Gratitude

A little boy kneeling by the side of the bed looked up to heaven and prayed, "And now, God, let me tell you about the things I'm not thankful for."

Happiness

"Folks are generally as happy as they make up their minds to be." (Abraham Lincoln)

Happiness

"The happiness of your life depends upon the character of your thoughts." (Marcus Aurelius)

Happiness

"Many persons have a wrong idea about what constitutes true happiness. It is not attained through self gratifications, but through fidelity to a worthy purpose." (Helen Keller)

Holiness

"The aim of reconciliation (to God) is holiness. Christ carried out His sacrificial work of reconciliation in order to present us to God, holy, unblemished, and irreproachable." (William Barclay, quoted by Max Anders, *The Good Life*, Dallas: Word Publishing, 1993, pp. 146-147.)

Holiness

"Holiness apart from Christlikeness is hollowness." (E. Stanley Jones)

Holy Spirit

"The greatest unused power in the world is the Holy Spirit of the living God." (A. J. Gordon)

Homemaker

Patrick M. Morley quotes Richard Kerr who wrote, "The most creative job in the world involves fashion, decorating, recreation, education, transportation, psychology, romance, cuisine, literature, art, economics, government, pediatrics, geriatrics, entertainment, maintenance, purchasing, law, religion, energy, and management. Anyone who can handle all those has to be somebody special. She is. She's a homemaker." (Patrick M. Morley, *Walking with Christ in the Details of Life*, Nashville: Thomas Nelson Publishers, 1992, p. 250.)

Honesty
Josh McDowell, writing in *Focus on the Family* magazine, discusses with parents the benefits of right choices for young people. He states that parents need to counter deceptive choices with the truth about honesty. He gives some excellent examples:
* Being honest protects from guilt and provides for a clear conscience and unbroken fellowship with God.
* Being honest protects from shame and provides a sense of accomplishment.
* Being honest protects from the cycle of deceit and builds a reputation of integrity and a "good name."
* Being honest protects from ruined relationships and provides for trusting relationships.

(*Focus on the Family*, Colorado Springs, Colo.: Focus on the Family Production, November, 1994, p. 4.)

Honesty
"Today I'm giving two examinations. One in trigonometry and the other in honesty," Dr. Madison Sarratt used to tell his class at Vanderbilt University each year. "I hope you will pass them both. If you must fail one, fail trigonometry. There are many good people in the world who can't pass trig, but there are no good people in the world who cannot pass a test of honesty." (Dr. Madison Sarratt from "Leadership")

Hope
"A leader is one who deals in hope." (Napoleon Bonaparte)

Human Freedom

"Authentic Wesleyan theology holds to a significantly different interpretation of the historical process. While God is still sovereign over the total process of history, He guides the process within the context of human freedom — this is synergism. Human choices are real and actually influence the course of history. Human beings are not mere pawns being moved about the chessboard by a master chessman and having no input into the gambits in which they participate." (H. Ray Dunning, editor, *The Second Coming*, Kansas City: Beacon Hill Press of Kansas City, 1995, p. 196.)

Involvement

"Football is 22 people on the field who desperately need rest and 22,000 people in the stands who desperately need exercise." (Bud Wilkerson)

Jealousy

Some things you just can't exaggerate from the Bible. Word has it that Eve would get so jealous of Adam that she would count his ribs every night when he got home from the garden!

Joy

It was difficult for the teacher, but the circumstances were a bit unusual. A kid in the class kept disrupting the whole classroom of other children with his "hallelujahs." He did it once too often and off he went to the principal's office. The busy principal gave the boy a geography book to look at, thinking that there was nothing worth a hallelujah on the pages. Suddenly, the principal heard a loud "hallelujah" and dashed over to see what made the boy get all excited.

He asked the boy what made him say, "Hallelujah." The boy replied, "I was just reading in this geography book about oceans, and I came to a sentence which says that the depth of some seas has not been discovered, and my Bible says that my sins have been cast into the depth of the sea — hallelujah!" (Leslie B. Flynn, *Come Alive With Illustrations*, Grand Rapids: Baker Book House, 1988, p. 157.)

Joy
Max Anders quotes Alexander Solzhenitsyn, "The only way to survive in prison is to abandon all expectations for this world and live for the next." Anders comments, "The only way to have consistent joy in this life is to place our values, our hopes, our expectations, and our affections in the next world, not this one." (Max Anders, *The Good Life*, Dallas: Word Publishing, 1993, p. 273.)

Joy
Joy is not the absence of suffering, but the presence of God.

Laughter
Laughter is the chimney sweep for the cinders of the heart.

Leadership
"Leadership is influence!" (John C. Maxwell)

Leadership
"A great leader takes people where they don't really want to go, but ought to be." (Rosalyn Carter)

Leadership
"Leadership is leaders inducing followers to act for certain goals that represent the values and motivations, the wants and needs, the aspirations and expectations of both leaders and followers. And the genius of leadership lies in the manner in which leaders see and act on their own and their followers' values and motivations." (James McGregor Burns)

Leadership
"A position does not give you followers, only subordinates." (John Gardner)

Leadership
"Great leaders inspire us to go places we would never go on our own and to attempt things we never thought we had in us." (Hans Finzel)

Leadership

A leader has two major characteristics: first, he is going someplace; second, he is capable of persuading others to travel with him.

Lie

"A lie stands on one leg, truth on two." (Benjamin Franklin)

Life

"If you had an hour to live and could make only one phone call, whom would you call, what would you say, and why are you waiting?" (Stephen Levine)

Life

Live each day as if it is your last; some day you will be right. (Stan Toler, *Pastor's Little Instruction Book*, Nashville: Brentwood Press, 1994, p. 154.)

Love

The great acts of love are usually done by those who humbly do small acts of kindness.

Love

"Alexander, Caesar, Charlemagne, and I myself have founded great empires ... But Jesus alone founded His empire upon love, and to this very day, millions would die for Him. Jesus Christ was more than a man." (Napoleon Bonaparte)

Love

Sign in a pet shop: "Love Guaranteed Forever." (Quoted by King Duncan)

Lust

A story is told that two monks traveling together in a rain storm in Japan talked about the importance of celibacy. The rain poured heavier and their path became pure mud. Coming around a bend in the road, they discovered a beautiful young woman in a lovely silk kimono unable to cross the intersection because of the muddy street. The monk, Tanzan, impulsively spoke to her saying, "Come on, young lady," and instinctively lifted her in his arms and carried her over the mud-soaked road. His traveling companion, Ekido, did not speak again on their walk until they reached their destination late that night. Once inside the lodge and in their room Ekido could no longer restrain himself and told Tanzan, "We monks don't go near females and especially not young and beautiful ones. It is dangerous! Why did you do that?"

Tanzan replied, "I left the girl there. Are you still carrying her?" (Simon Tugwell, Job and Shawchuck, *A Guide to Prayer*, Nashville: The Upper Room, 1983, pp. 208-209.)

Marriage

A minister advertised for a man to help him with house chores. The following morning a nicely-dressed young man rang the doorbell.

"Can you start the fire and get breakfast by seven o'clock?" inquired the pastor.

"I guess so," answered the young man.

"What about the silver, can you polish it? How about the dishes? Can you keep the house neat and tidy?"

"Say, preacher," said the young man, "I came here to see about getting married — but if it's going to be as much work as all that you can count me out right now!" (King Duncan, *Lively Illustrations for Effective Preaching*, Knoxville: Seven Worlds Corporation, 1987, p. 264.)

Money

Many years ago a newspaper office offered a prize for the best definition of "money." Hundreds competed, but the winning definition stated it best.

"Money is a universal provider of everything but happiness; and a passport to everywhere but heaven."

Mortality

Wade Clark Roof, a professor at the University of California, Santa Barbara, is quoted as saying that this generation is facing up to the reality that jogging, liposuction, and all the brown rice in China cannot keep us young forever: "As our bodies fall apart, as they weaken and sag, it speaks of mortality." Roof goes on to say that Baby Boomers "are at a point in their lives where they sense the need for spirituality, but they don't know where to get it." (Greg Laurie, *Life—Any Questions*, Dallas: Word Publishing, 1995, p. 60.)

Morality

Arthur Berry was a very successful jewel thief back in the Roaring Twenties. He hobnobbed with the famous and rich of Boston's elite, but he did his hobnobbing at night when the folks weren't home. It is said that Berry's visits were a status symbol among the ladies of Boston's upper class. His status-orientation wasn't as intriguing to the police. He was making one of his nightly calls when the police caught up with him and shot him three times. He fell through a glass window, shattered glass stuck in his body, and he lay on the ground in horrible pain. While lying there he came to a conclusion, "I ain't going to do this anymore."

Arthur Berry went to prison for twenty years. After serving his time he moved to a quiet New England town. There he became a respectable citizen. Eventually word leaked out to the press that this notorious jewel thief had settled in the tiny New England town — and the nation's media services arrived in great numbers. One young reporter asked him, "Mr. Berry, you stole from a lot of rich people in your life as a jewel thief. Let me ask you a question. From whom did you steal the most?"

Without a moment's hesitation he replied, "That's the easiest question I've ever been asked. The individual from whom I stole the most was a man named Arthur Berry. I could have done anything, been an executive on Wall Street, a successful business man, or anything I wanted to be, but I utilized my God-given talents and developed them illegitimately. I could have made it big in business but I spent two-thirds of my adult life behind bars." (King Duncan, *Lively Illustrations for Effective Preaching*, Knoxville: Seven Worlds Corporation, 1987, pp. 308-309.)

Mother

"The most glorious sight that one ever sees beneath the stars is the sight of worthy motherhood." (George W. Truett, quoted by Terri Gibbs, compiler, *Heartstrings of Laughter and Love*, Dallas: Word Book Publishing, 1997.)

Mother

God could not be everywhere, and therefore, he made mothers. (Jewish proverb)

Mother

"A mother keeps a vigil at the bedside of her sick child. The world calls it 'fatigue' but she calls it love." (Bishop Fulton J. Sheen, quoted by Terri Gibbs, compiler, *Heartstrings of Laughter and Love*, Dallas: Word Book Publishing, 1997.)

Mother

"Judicious mothers will always keep in mind that they are the first book read, and the last put aside, in every child's library." (Lenox Redmond, quoted by Terri Gibbs, compiler, *Heartstrings of Laughter and Love*, Dallas: Word Book Publishing, 1997.)

Mother's Day

"To Mother-in-law ... Mother's Day brings a wonderful opportunity to thank you for all the time and effort you took in raising the perfect partner — the one who married me." (Mother's Day greeting card, Paramount Cards, Inc.)

Motivation

King Duncan, in his book *Amusing Grace*, relates a story about a man during the early twentieth century who traveled from city to city to put on a "side show" to earn a living. One of the features was an elephant trained to follow his instructions and no one else's.

One day he arrived in a small town and gathered a large crowd around him and then challenged anyone to try to make the elephant "shake his head from side to side as if he were saying, 'No.' " It cost one dollar per try. Several people tried unsuccessfully and the man started to pick up his cash. Just then a young boy asked if he could try. "Sure, put your dollar with the rest," replied the sarcastic man. When the boy put the money on the pile of ones he then promptly left and went behind a building. He quickly returned carrying a 2 x 4 in his hand. He stood directly in front of the elephant, showed him the 2 x 4 and promptly hit the elephant alongside the head, causing the elephant to shake its head from side to side.

The boy took the money and left as an angry and frustrated animal trainer yelled at him.

A year later the showman returned, this time with the elephant trained to shake its head "Yes," and made the same challenge. That same little boy showed up and laid his dollar on the pile of dollars. He stood again directly in front of the mammoth beast and carried a 2 x 4 and showed the elephant the board. He then asked, "Hey, elephant, remember me?" The elephant shook his head "Yes!"

King Duncan said, "That elephant was motivated to remember!" What does it take to get you motivated? (King Duncan, *Amusing Grace*, Knoxville: Seven Worlds Corporation, 1993, p. 239.)

Nation
"No nation ever had a better friend than the mother who taught her children to pray." (Anonymous, quoted by Terri Gibbs, compiler, *Heartstrings of Laughter and Love*, Dallas: Word Book Publishing, 1997.)

New Year
"I said to the man who stood at the gate, 'Give me light that I may tread safely into the unknown.' And he replied, 'Go out into the darkness and put thy hand into the hand of God. That shall be to thee better than a light and safer than a known way.'" (Anonymous)

New Year
"Farewell, Old Year, with goodness crowned, a Hand divine hath set thy bound; welcome the New Year which shall bring fresh blessings from My Lord and King. The Old we leave with just a tear, the New we enter without fear." (Anonymous)

Obedience
"Partial obedience is total rebellion." (Anonymous)

Obedience
"The mind of Christ is a servant mind: a mind that puts obedience to God above everything else; a mind that puts others before self. It is a mind that does not insist on being 'number one.' " (Kay Arthur, *His Imprint My Expression*, Eugene, Ore.: Harvest House Publishers, 1993, p. 104.)

Parenthood
"Parents who care unselfishly for their children, who provide for them spiritually as well as materially, are performing an invaluable service. They are helping to create a stable and secure world." (Robert McCracken, quoted by Terri Gibbs, compiler, *Heartstrings of Laughter and Love*, Dallas: Word Book Publishing, 1997.)

Patience
"Since God is eternal and I am immortal, I can wait." (J. B. Chapman)

Peace
"Peace is not the absence of tension; it is the presence of Jesus." (Jarrell W. Garsee, *Come Ye Apart*, Kansas City: Nazarene Publishing House, December-February, 1997-1998, p. 31.)

Persistence
Persistence transforms vision into reality.

Politics
"Nothing is politically right which is morally wrong." (Daniel O'Connell)

Prayer

"Satan laughs at our toiling and mocks our tryings, but he shakes when he sees the weakest saint of God on his knees." (Paul A. Cedar, quoted by Bill Bright, *The Coming Revival*, Orlando, Fla.: New Life Publications, 1995, p. 106.)

Prayer

"A prayer is nothing but a cry of helplessness: 'God help me.' When we ask on that level, God promises to give." (Ray Stedman, quoted by Max Anders, *The Good Life*, Dallas: Word Publishing, 1993, p. 71.)

Prayer

"He who labors as he prays lifts his heart to God with his hands." (Bernard of Clairvaux)

Prayer

"Other things being equal, your growth and mine into the likeness of our Lord and Savior Jesus Christ will be in exact proportion to the time and to the heart we put into prayer." (R. A. Torrey)

Prayer

"What the church needs today is not more machinery or better, nor new organizations or more and novel methods, but men whom the Holy Ghost can use — men of prayer, men mighty in prayer. The Holy Ghost does not flow through methods, but through men. He does not come on machinery, but on men. He does not anoint plans, but men — men of prayer." (E. M. Bounds, quoted by Eleanor Doan, editor, *The Speaker's Sourcebook*, Grand Rapids: Zondervan Publishing House, 1975, p. 191.)

Prayer

Greg Laurie wrote that the literal definition of the word "pray" in Luke 11:1 is "to wish forward." He commented that prayer should not be merely lip service, or a grocery list of requests, but a genuine expression of our desires to seek God's will for our lives. "Our prayer should reflect our desire to move forward in our walk with Christ." (Greg Laurie, *Every Day With Jesus*, Eugene, Ore.: Harvest House Publishers, 1993, p. 216.)

Prayer
"Prayer is an offering up of our desires unto God, for things agreeable to His will, in the name of Christ, with confession of our sins, and thankful acknowledgment of His mercies." (Westminster Catechism)

Prayer
"Prayer is a powerful thing; for God has bound and tied himself there unto." (Martin Luther)

Prayer
"Prayer is not conquering God's reluctance, but taking hold of God's willingness." (Phillips Brooks)

Pride
This story of Muhammad Ali in his heyday is told by Charles Swindoll in his book, *Hope Again*.

As heavyweight champion of the world, Muhammad Ali was pompous and a bit testy. He had taken his seat on a giant 747 as it began taxiing toward the runway. A flight attendant walked by and saw that the champ had not fastened his seat belt.

The attendant told Ali, "Please fasten your seat belt."

He looked up and snapped, "Superman don't need no seat belt, lady!"

Without missing a beat she peered at him and shot back, "Superman don't need no plane ... so buckle up!" (Charles Swindoll, *Hope Again*, Dallas: Word Publishing, 1996, p. 257.)

Problems
"The man who has no problems is out of the game." (Elbert Hubbard)

Progress

Slow progress is always better than no progress at all.

Revival

Former President Herbert Hoover said, "This country needs a rebirth of a great spiritual force, which has been impaired by cynicism and weakened by foreign infections."

Revival

"Depending solely on our own efforts to produce religious revival is like propelling a boat by puffing with our own breath at the sails." (Arthur T. Pierson)

Ridicule

Two men strolled down the street when a pretty co-ed passed by them. One said, "Why, that gal smiled at me."

His red-headed friend chuckled at him: "Don't be too surprised; the first time I saw you, I laughed out loud!" (James Dyke, quoted by Michael Hodgin, editor, *The Pastor's Story File*, Vol. 14, No. 1, Platteville, Colo.: Saratoga Press, November, 1997, p. 8.)

Sacrifice

"Remember that when your back is against a wall — His back was against a cross." (Church sign board)

Salvation

The first shocks brought terror to everyone that December day in 1988. People weren't ready for the horror that befell them in Soviet Armenia. Susanna Petrosyan and her four-year-old daughter Gayaney lived in a 36-story apartment building that was reduced to a mound of rubble. All of the brick, mortar, steel, and wood was flattened like a pancake on the Armenian ground. Hundreds of people were killed instantly while others lingered to life. Susanna and Gayaney were alive — spared yet buried alive. They were squeezed in an eighteen-inch gap between the floor and the collapsed ceiling.

Susanna lay on her back for the first few hours of their tribulation trying to calm her daughter's fears. In the deep recesses of her heart she despaired of being rescued before they both perished. Yet, she refused to quit her struggle for life. Confined to a small space as she groped for food or water, her fingers discovered an object of hope: a half-filled jar of fruit jam. With her fingers, she fed the sweet stuff to Gayaney.

Gayaney later pleaded weakly for something to quench her thirst. Her mother hushed her crying for a little while. There was no water.

"Mommy, I'm thirsty," repeated Gayaney.

Night came, then day, then a blending of each. There was no more food, no water, no help. Gayaney became too weak to plead for water. Dehydration would soon set in if something wasn't done and done quickly. Susanna did the only thing she could think of that would save her child. She broke the empty jar and used a broken piece to slit her finger. Then she placed her bleeding finger in Gayaney's mouth.

Repeatedly Susanna applied this process sustaining her daughter's life with her own blood.

Eight grueling days of horror, boredom, hunger, and thirst until finally Susanna's husband and a band of rescue workers clawed their way into that narrow living tomb. Susanna had not only conquered her ordeal, but she kept Gayaney alive with the sacrifice of her own blood. (Ron Lee Davis, *Becoming a Whole Person in a Broken World*, Grand Rapids: Discovery House Publishers, 1990, pp. 93-94.)

Salvation

Author Randal Denny tells the story of a simple-minded, illiterate man in England who was converted at a Salvation Army meeting. He began attending the meetings. His wife wasn't exactly clear as to what had happened, but she knew he was happy and he did his best to make her happy as well. One day he returned home from the Salvation Army meeting rather ruffled.

She quizzed, "What's wrong?"

"They all have red sweaters," he answered, "and I don't have a red sweater." So she went to work and knitted him one.

The first time he wore his new red sweater, he returned home sad again.

"Now what's wrong?" his wife asked.

"They all have yellow writing on their red sweaters," he answered. Unable to read, she still promised him that she would embroider some yellow writing onto his red sweater. She ventured across the street to a shop window, copied some letters, and embroidered them on his red sweater.

Coming home after the next meeting he was all smiles. The wife asked, "Did they like the sweater?"

"Yes," he answered.

"What did they say about the writing?" questioned his wife.

He replied that they liked the writing on his sweater better than the writing on theirs.

Unknowingly she had embroidered on his red sweater, "This business is under new management."

Dr. Denny commented, "We celebrate that we are under new management. We can resign as the nervous rulers of our puny universe and rest in the Lord who has given us new life."

Truly we are under new management! (Randal Earl Denny, *The Kingdom, the Power, the Glory*, Kansas City: Beacon Hill Press of Kansas City, 1997, pp. 140-141.)

Satan

"I believe Satan to exist for two reasons: first, the Bible says so, and second, I've done business with him." (Dwight L. Moody)

Self-control

Ron Boehme states that he remembers coming home from school and often being faced with a true test of self-control. The scent of freshly-baked chocolate chip cookies would hit him in the nostrils.

Racing into the kitchen he would see a plate of them sitting on the counter, but his mom would be at the sink cleaning up the dirty pans.

"Don't even think about touching those cookies," she would warn.

Boehme said, "It was like a shot to the stomach when she told me that."

It would take all that he could muster to keep his grubby little hands off those cookies.

"Sometimes, when she left the room I'd borrow a cookie," he confessed. "When I got caught, my parents showed me another form of control called 'shelf control,' in which they applied a hairbrush to my bottom shelf!"

He brought the point to bear when he wrote: "My concept of self-control was backward, I thought self-control was 'resisting temptation or evil.' Later in life, I discovered that this is not the proper emphasis. Self-control is not primarily resisting wrong. It is possessing right with such conviction that resisting wrong is the natural result ... When we're committed to holy living, the resistance to temptation becomes an automatic response to a choice already made. That's why goodness in the heart must precede self-control." (Ron Boehme, *If God Has A Plan For My Life, Why Can't I Find It?*, Seattle, Wash.: YMAM Publishing, 1992, pp. 64-65.)

Service

"Make us worthy, Lord, to serve those throughout the world who die in poverty and hunger. Give them through our hands this day their daily bread." (Mother Teresa of Calcutta, quoted in *Come Ye Apart*, Kansas City: Nazarene Publishing House, December-February, 1997-1998, p. 85.)

Service

"God lifts us out of the mere mechanics of service into His blessed dynamics." (Henrietta C. Mears)

Serving

"Everybody can be great. Because anybody can serve. You don't have to have a college degree to serve ... You don't have to know about Plato and Aristotle to serve. You don't have to know Einstein's theory of relativity to serve ... You only need a heart full of grace. A soul generated by love." (Martin Luther King, Jr.)

Smile
"All people smile in the same language." (Anonymous)

Spiritual Irresponsibility
On the bulletin board of a church. "Sunday at 11 a.m.: Forward with Christ; Wednesday at 7:30, the Midweek Retreat." (Gerald Kennedy, quoted by Charles L. Wallis, editor, *Speaker's Illustrations for Special Days*, Grand Rapids: Baker Book House, 1956, p. 71.)

Spiritual Life
Oswald Chambers wrote, "The best misuse of the spiritual life is not its ecstasies but its obedience." (Albert Wells, *Inspiring Quotations*, Nashville: Thomas Nelson, 1988, p. 143.)

Stewardship
Lawrence L. Durgin wrote: "Christian stewardship is the matching of gift for matchless gift: our life and its whole substance for the gift of perfect love. And though God's Son and His precious death are matchless — in the strange economy of God our gift returned is made sufficient. My all for His all. Stewardship is your commitment: the asking of God to take you back unto Himself — all that you have and all that you are." (Frank S. Mead, editor, *12,000 Religious Quotations*, Grand Rapids: Baker Book House, 1989, p. 427.)

Stress And Pain
Charles Swindoll tells how God helps train us through adjustment to irritation and pain.

He relates that pearls are a great illustration of pain and the adjustments one has to make in life. Swindoll shares that the shell of the oyster gets pierced and an alien object enters, lodging itself inside. Upon the forced entry of that article every resource within the diminutive oyster rushes to the blemish and begins releasing healing fluids that would otherwise remain dormant for the life of the oyster. After a period of time the pesky intruder is covered and the wound is healed and transformed into a pearl. Swindoll writes, "No other gem has so fascinating a history. It is the symbol of stress — a healed wound ... a precious, tiny jewel conceived through irritation, born of adversity, nursed by adjustments. Had there been no wounding, no irritating interruption, there could have been no pearl. Some oysters are never wounded ... and those who seek for gems toss them aside, fit only for stew." (Charles Swindoll, *Growing Strong In The Seasons Of Life*, Portland, Ore.: Multnomah Press, 1983, p. 164.)

Stress — Good And Bad

Basically, there are two types of stress: distress, which isn't good, and eustress, which is good. Eustress motivates us to action as a positive force of energy driving us from within. It is motivation to do our best and to carry out our goals and purposes. Distress is destructive either/or physically and emotionally by producing a negative pressure in life. The truth is both types exhaust us physically, but one leaves us with a weary frown while the other a fulfilled smile.

Jay Strack comments that "life is a bountiful rose garden of beauty — right down to the thorns and fertilizer!" (Jay Strack, *Above and Beyond*, Dallas: Word Publishing, 1994, pp. 43-44.)

Success

"Where success is concerned, people are not measured in inches or pounds, or college degrees, or family background. They are measured by the size of their thinking. How big we think determines the size of our accomplishments." (David Schwartz and Stan Toler, *Minute Motivators*, Kansas City: Beacon Hill Press of Kansas City, 1996, p. 16.)

Suffering

Max Lucado, writing in *Moody Magazine* in November, 1995, tells the story of two maestros who attended a concert to hear a promising young soprano. One of the maestros commented on the purity of her voice.

The other responded, "Yes, but she will sing better once her heart is broken."

Sympathy
"Sympathy is your pain in my heart." (Anonymous child)

Teamwork
"A great manager has a knack for making players think they're better than they think they are. Once you learn how good you really are, you never settle for playing less than your best." (Reggie Jackson, quoted by Peg Anderson, compiler, *Winning with Teamwork*, Lombard, Ill.: Successories Library, 1992, p. 14.)

Thought
"Ours is the age which is proud of machines that think and suspicious of men who try to." (Howard H. Jones)

Thoughts
"You are today where your thoughts have brought you. You will be tomorrow where your thoughts take you." (James Allen)

Training
"A true mother is not merely a provider, housekeeper, comforter, or companion. A true mother is primarily and essentially a trainer." (Terri Gibbs, compiler, *Heartstrings of Laughter and Love*, Dallas: Word Book Publishing, 1997.)

Trials
"Great hearts can only be made by great troubles." (G. H. Spurgeon)

Trials
"Afflictions color your life, but you choose the color." (John Maxwell)

Triumph

"These are the times that try men's souls. The summer soldier and the sunshine patriot will, in this crisis, shrink from the service of their country, but he that stands it now deserves the love and thanks of man and woman. Tyranny, like hell, is not easily conquered; yet we have this consolation with us, that the harder the conflict, the more glorious the triumph." (Thomas Paine)

Unity

"Tying two cats' tails together does not necessarily constitute unity." (Anonymous)

Unwanted

"I have come more and more to realize that being unwanted is the worst disease that any human being can ever experience. Nowadays we have found medicine for leprosy, and lepers can be cured. There's medicine for TB, and the consumption can be cured. But for being unwanted, except there are willing hands to serve and there's a loving heart to love, I don't think this terrible disease can be cured." (Mother Teresa, quoted in *God's Treasury of Virtues*, Tulsa: Honor Books, 1995, p. 232.)

Virginity

Charles Colson, in his book, *A Dangerous Grace*, tells that *Glamour* magazine made the shocking discovery that many of its readers were virgins.

Colson said it started when the magazine asked its readers to respond to the question, "Are there any virgins left out there?" Two thousand women wrote in to tell the magazine that they were virgins ... and proud of it. The magazine summarized the responses in a March 1992 article titled, "2,000 Virgins: They're Not Who You Think." The article went on to say that the women who wrote were intelligent, "with-it" young women who were articulate and knew what they wanted in life.

They had simply chosen not to have sex outside of marriage.

Their letters disclosed that it is not an easy choice to make in these days. These women told of being teased, humiliated, ridiculed — made to feel like freaks. Some of those ladies sent pictures to prove they're really just normal human beings.

Colson said that the women wrote that they took their stands for a variety of reasons.

He states that all of them listed AIDS and other sexually-transmitted diseases as good reasons to remain chaste. Others said that they didn't want to be pressured into sex by peers and media. Many said sex is too meaningful for a casual relationship. One woman wrote: "A lot of feeling, trust, and intimacy are put into a relationship once sex is involved." That was her reason to save herself for the right man. Other respondents warned that sex outside marriage loses its deep meaning. One woman wrote to *Glamour* that, "Sex is expressing love — and you can't possibly love a new person every few months."

These women did not express a low view of sex. On the contrary, they saw it as something with intense meaning and a committed relationship of marriage. One letter-writer expressed it very well: "God doesn't forbid sex before marriage because He wants to put us in a box with a list of rules and no fun. No, it's because He wants the best for us." She hit at the core of the issue. Colson writes, "God's laws are not capricious or arbitrary. They tell us who we are and what is truly best for us." (Charles Colson, *A Dangerous Grace*, Dallas: Word Book Publishing, 1994, pp. 200-201.)

Vision

"One does not discover new lands without consenting to lose sight of the shore for a very long time." (Andre Gide, quoted by Jay Strack, *Above and Beyond*, Dallas: Word Publishing, 1994, p. 75.)

Vision

Walt Kallestad, in his outstanding book, *The Everyday, Anytime Guide to Christian Leadership*, tells about a visit to Strasbourg, France, where he delivered four lectures at St. Nicholas Church. It was in this church that John Calvin was a minister, Martin Luther preached, and Albert Schweitzer was the Minister of Music. He writes:

"Wow — what a lineup! There had been people of great vision in this church, yet only five centuries after they opened, the church doors were locked. No one came any longer; only pigeons ever saw the inside. How did that happen? It happened because the vision or purpose for the church was lost. Without a vision, the church literally perished."

But that is not the end of the story of the St. Nicholas Church! Not by a long shot. In 1992, the local bishop requested that any pastor who had a vision for this empty, historic church building could submit a vision plan. It seems that one pastor was equal to the challenge of his bishop. Eventually permission was granted for the pastor to carry out his vision plan. When Pastor Kallestad delivered his four lectures in that church he said he was excited to see approximately 350 people jammed into the building. He says that the church has the largest attendance of any Lutheran church in France.

It really is true that with a vision people prosper — without a vision the people perish. God help us to catch a vision for our local church whatever city, town, or village we minister in today! (Walt Kallestad, *The Everyday, Anytime Guide to Christian Leadership*, Minneapolis: Augsburg, 1994, pp. 25-26.)

Vision
"The way you see your future determines your thinking today, and your thinking today determines your performance today." (Anthony Campolo)

Vision
"Visions are born of care and are given form and substance through added preparation." (Paul S. Rees)

Vision
"To grasp and hold a vision — that is the essence of successful leadership." (Ronald Reagan)

Word
"A word is dead when it is said, some say. I say it just begins to live that day." (Emily Dickinson)

Work
"If a man is called to be a street sweeper, he should sweep streets even as Michelangelo paints, or Beethoven composed music, or Shakespeare wrote poetry. He should sweep streets so well that all hosts of heaven and earth will pause to say, 'Here lived a great street sweeper who did his job well.' " (Martin Luther King, Jr.)

World
We cannot have a better world without first having a better man. (*Newsweek*)

World
The world is a globe that revolves on its taxes.

Worship
"Satan doesn't care what we worship, as long as we don't worship God." (Dwight L. Moody)

Worship
"Worship is not performance — it is participation." (Robert Webber)

Worship
"A man can no more diminish God's glory by refusing to worship Him than a lunatic can put out the sun by scribbling the word 'darkness' on the walls of his cell." (C. S. Lewis)

Mom Is More Than A 3-Letter Word

Inspirational thoughts, sayings, and ideas for Moms
- "Heaven is at the feet of mothers." (Roebuck)
- "All that I am, my mother made me." (John Quincy Adams)
- "I think it must somewhere be written that the virtues of mothers shall occasionally be visited on their children, as well as the sins of fathers." (Charles Dickens)
- A virtuous woman will have "her children arise and call her blessed." (Proverbs 31:28 NIV)
- A beautiful stained-glass window in New York state has the inscription, "To a sainted mother." Let that be your inscription.
- Paul Lewis suggested that mothers ought to take photos of the children doing things right — daily chores, cleaning their rooms, grooming a pet, doing homework, helping someone. Then set aside special pages in the family album for these snapshots to get out on those "not so pleasant" days.
- One Mother's Day card read, "Now that we have a mature, adult relationship there is something I'd like to tell you. 'You're still the first person I think of when I fall down and go boom!'"
- An old Jewish proverb says, "A child without a mother is like a door without a knob."
- A little girl was shown pictures of her mommy and daddy on their wedding day. She asked her father, "Daddy, is that the day you got mom to come and work for us?"
- "An ounce of mother is worth a pound of clergy." (Spanish proverb)
- "The most important occupation on the earth for a woman is to be a real mother to her children. It does not have much glory in it; there is a lot of grit and grime, but there is no greater place of ministry, position, or power than that of a mother." (Phil Wisenhut)
- "Mothers ... fill places so great that there isn't an angel in heaven who wouldn't be glad to give a bushel of diamonds to come down here and take their place." (Billy Sunday)

- Mothers help set the morals that develop character in their children.
- Moms are like lighthouses — they always send out light.
- Mothers of the world can help produce an upsurge of vital, God-centered, intelligently grounded power through prayer!
- Remember when charity was a virtue instead of an IRS deduction?
- Prejudice is the mother of ignorance and the sister of hate.
- Most moms are aware that happiness is a spot between too little and too much that their kids often visit.
- The philosopher, Immanuel Kant, said that the dove might consider air resistance a problem, something to overcome, but without it the doves couldn't fly. Every mom has met with some of that "air resistance problem," but that's what makes her fly.
- Somebody's mother once said, "If you're wondering when middle age begins — watch out, it's begun already!"
- Moms never creep when they can soar!
- Most mothers resemble what Robert Louis Stevenson says about quiet minds, that they "cannot be perplexed or frightened, but go on in fortune or misfortune at their own pace like the ticking of a clock during a thunderstorm."
- Mothers know that the best medicine chest for ailing families is the Bible.
- It takes courage to overcome discouragement.
- You are unable to shoulder the cross and hate at the same time.
- It must have been a wise mother who said, "When we die, we leave behind us all we have and take with us all we are."
- How many mothers have come to grief in their indecisions?
- The best discipline is the greatest mercy.
- No mother is so old as those who have outlived their enthusiasm for children.
- Christian mothers realize that faith is the belief that we are loved by God.
- Eve: "Do you really love me?"
  Adam: "Who else?"
- What this country needs are more Christian mothers!
- Your expression is the portrait of your spirit.

- Without God, the world is simply a place where people sit and listen to each other moan and groan.
- A mother's righteousness is her beauty in its best light.
- A habit, if it is not resisted, soon becomes a necessity.
- "A mother's heart is the precious porcelain of human clay."
- A mother's love is never afraid of giving too much.
- Mother is really a four-letter word — LOVE.
- A wise mother teaches her children to seek God first.
- "Those who know your name will trust in you, for you, Lord, have never forsaken those who seek you." (Psalm 9:10 NIV)
- On May 7, 1914, Thomas J. Heflin of Alabama and Senator Sheppard of Texas introduced into Congress a resolution for a Mother's Day with these words, "Whereas the service rendered by the American mother is the greatest source of the country's strength and inspiration...."
- "Youth fades, love droops, the leaves of friendship fall; a mother's secret hope outlives them all." (Oliver Wendell Holmes)
- "One lamp, thy mother's love amid the stars shall lift its pure flame changeless, and before the throne of God burn eternally." (N. P. Willis)
- In *Speaker's Treasury of Stories for All Occasions*, Herbert Prochnow tells: Aunt Betty came up the walk and said to her small nephew, "Good morning, Willie. Is your mother in?" "Sure she is," replied Willie. "D'you s'pose I'd be workin' in the garden on a Saturday morning if she wasn't?"
- "God could not be everywhere, and so He made mothers." (Jewish proverb)
- "Mother is the name for God in the lips and hearts of little children." (William Makepeace Thackeray)
- "The sweetest face in all the world to me, Set in a frame of shining golden hair,
With eyes whose language is fidelity; That is my mother. Is she not most fair?" (May Riley Smith)
- An old-timer is one who can remember when a baby-sitter was called mother.
- "I don't think there are enough devils in hell to take a young person from the arms of a godly mother." (Billy Sunday)

- Henry Ward Beecher: "The mother's heart is the child's schoolroom."
- "The sweetest sounds to mortals given are heard in mother, home, and heaven." (William Brown)
- "The future destiny of the child is always the work of the mother." (Napoleon Bonaparte)
- President Abraham Lincoln is credited with saying, "All that I am or hope to be, I owe to my angel mother."
- "Of all the men I have known, I cannot recall one whose mother did her level best for him when he was little, who did not turn out well when he grew up." (Frances Parkinson Keyes)
- The noblest mother is the public good.
- "Summer camps — those places where little boys go for mother's vacation." (Jacob Braude)
- Motherhood is woman's greatest achievement.
- "Simply having children does not make mothers." (A. Shedd in *Salt from My Attic*)
- "Children are the anchors that hold a mother to life." (Sophocles)
- "The hand that rocks the cradle is the hand that rules the world." (William Wallace)
- In this cold and lifeless world no one has so deep and strong a love except that which is found in a mother's heart.
- "A man never sees all that his mother has been to him until it's too late to let her know that he sees it." (W. D. Howells)
- "If you would reform the world from its errors and vices, begin by enlisting the mothers." (C. Simmons)
- There is no sweeter name than — Mother.
- "No language can express the power and beauty and heroism and majesty of a mother's love. It shrinks not where man cowers, and grows strong where man faints, and over the wastes of worldly fortune sends the radiance of quenchless fidelity like a star in heaven." (E. H. Chapin)
- "A mother's love is indeed the golden link that binds youth to age; and he is still a child, however time may have furrowed his cheek, or silvered his brow, who can yet recall, with softened heart, the fine devotion, or the gentle chidings, of the best friend that God ever gives us." (Bover)

- A mother's love is the steadfast devotion to her children.
- Mothers put the music in our hearts.
- There is no stare like a mother's stare.
- Motherhood holds the keys to the soul.
- There is no joy like the joy that a mother puts in the heart of her children.
- Everything else may pass away, but not a mother's love.
- There is no heartbeat like the heartbeat of a mother.
- No language can express a mother's hope.
- "Men are what their mothers make them." (Ralph Waldo Emerson)
- To lead the world to reformation one begins by enlisting the mothers.
- No touch is like a mother's touch.
- I believe that the angels speak in soft tones when they speak the name of "Mother."
- Smiles break out when mother comes.
- Some children were asked if they knew anyone who was always good. One replied, "Yes, sir, I know one — my mom."
- A frustrated mother of three very lively boys went to the manager of the local grocery and begged, "Isn't there some cereal that will sap their energy?"
- "Automation: a technological process that performs all the work while we just sit there. When we were kids, this process was called — Mother." (King Duncan)
- The joy of motherhood is what a mom experiences when the kids have gone to bed.
- One new mom wrote back to her mother that she had worked without ceasing from son-up to son-down!
- "A mother never realizes that her children are no longer children." (Holbrook Jackson)
- "Every mother is like Moses. She does not enter the promised land; she prepares a world she will not see." (Pope Paul VI)
- "What the mother sings to the cradle goes all the way down to the coffin." (Henry Beecher)
- "A mother is not a person to lean on, but a person to make leaning unnecessary." (Dorothy Herbert)

- A mother needs to teach her children that a basic value system comes from God.
- Everyone else may desert you, but not your mom!
- We need to be patient with our mothers in the same way that God is patient with us.
- "He gives power to the tired and worn out, and strength to the weak." (Isaiah 40:29 TLB)
- A good mother is sunshine in a house.
- A mother's praise has outstanding effects upon children.
- A mother's prayers will help diminish a child's cares.
- "Love is patient, love is kind. It does not envy, it does not boast, it is not proud. Love never fails." (1 Corinthians 13:4, 8a NIV)
- Create good memories for your children along with good habits.
- "In everything set them an example by doing what is good." (Titus 2:7 NIV)
- A mother should never make differences between her children, but love them all.

101 Tips For Holy Living In An Unholy World

- "Holy, holy, holy is the Lord Almighty; the whole earth is full of his glory." (Isaiah 6:3)
- The Holy Spirit is not an "it," but a personality of the Trinity.
- Don't say, "No," to the Spirit.
- For God did not call us to be impure, but to live a holy life. (Paul of Tarsus)
- "God the Spirit, Guide and Guardian, Wind-sped flame and hovering Dove, Breath of life and voice of prophets, Sign of blessing, pow'r of life: Give to those who lead your people fresh anointing of your grace...." (Carl P. Daw, Jr., "God the Spirit, Guide and Guardian," *Sing To The Lord*, Lillenas Publishing Co., Kansas City, Mo., 1993, p. 780.)
- "I will ask the Father, and He will give you another Counselor to be with you forever — the Spirit of Truth." (John 14:16)
- God's Spirit wants to empower you for service — Today!
- Holiness unto the Lord is more than a thought ... it is a lifestyle.
- The greatest benefit of holiness is that it results in eternal life.
- It is God's will that you should be filled with His Spirit and be controlled by His righteousness.
- "The Comforter has come! The Comforter has come! The Holy ghost from heav'n, the Father's promise giv'n! O spread the tidings 'round wher-ever man is found: The Comforter has come!" (Frank Bottome, 1890, in *Sing To The Lord*, Lillenas Publishing Co., Kansas City, Mo., 1993, pp. 291-292.)
- Holiness is wholeness — the wholeness of Christ in the whole of life for the whole of eternity.
- A holy life has a voice. It speaks when the tongue is silent, and is either a continual attraction or a perpetual rejection.
- "He who has the Holy Spirit in his heart and the Scripture in his hands has all he needs." (Alexander MacLaren)
- My human best filled with the Spirit's best is a tremendous motto for life.

- "The Holy Spirit is God at work." (Dwight L. Moody)
- "To be sound in faith and holy in life — this is the kernel of Christianity." (Augustine)
- "Holiness is not a series of do's and don'ts, but a conformity to God's character in the very depths of our being. This conformity is possible only as we are united with Christ." (Jerry Bridges)
- A "yes" to God is a "no" to things that hurt His Holiness.
- Being a friend of God is the essence of holiness.
- The carnal person is overcome by the world, while the holy person overcomes the world through the power of the Spirit.
- "While the title to eternal life is given to us in our justification, the Lord leads us into the possession of eternal life along the way of holiness." (Norman Shepherd)
- "The first priority of my life is to be holy, and the second goal of my life is to be a scholar." (John Wesley)
- Holiness is not a place to linger, but a pathway to walk.
- Jesus put a great emphasis on the work of the Holy Spirit and the necessary power and presence He offers; it would be very foolish for the church not to emphasize the work of the Spirit.
- The Holy Spirit was not given to you to make you rich, famous, or spectacular, but to equip you for the task of life.
- "Just as the fluid in the eye keeps the dirt out of the eyes, so the constant cleansing presence of the Holy Spirit will keep the filth of the world out of the heart." (Myron Boyd)
- Methods, plans, and human efforts are futile without the inspiration of the Holy Spirit.
- "If a person is filled with the Holy Spirit, his witness will not be optional or mandatory — it will be inevitable." (Richard Halverson)
- Do not pray for more of the Holy Spirit, for He does not come as puzzle, but as a whole picture.
- The Holy Spirit's passion is to glorify Jesus as Lord.
- Christ's church does not move by pushing itself harder, but simply opening itself to the full potential of the Spirit.

- "I do not find in the Old Testament or in the New Testament, neither in Christian biography, in church history, nor in personal Christian testimonies the experience of any person who was ever filled with the Holy Ghost and who didn't know it." (A. W. Tozer)
- Holiness is a life of Christ-centered choices, evidenced by a life-centered obedience.
- A holiness lifestyle does not dissolve personality conflicts, but it definitely helps to cope with them.
- "While holiness does not make it impossible for you to sin, the experience does make it impossible not to sin." (Arlo F. Newell)
- The distinctives of holiness include: a separation from sin, a dedication to God, a call to service.
- "Pardon is not enough; we want sanctification. We beseech Thee, let the weeds that grow in the seed plot of our soul be cut up by the roots ... We would lead consecrated lives, for we are persuaded that we only live as we live unto God, that aught else is but trifling." (Charles H. Spurgeon)
- "The fruit of the Spirit is love, joy, peace, patience, gentleness, goodness, faithfulness, and self-control." (Galatians 5:22-23)
- "For God did not give us a spirit of timidity, but a spirit of power, of love, and of self-discipline." (2 Timothy 1:7)
- The Holy Spirit gives love, inspires eternal hope, and sets the spiritual captive free.
- "I should as soon attempt to raise flowers if there were no atmosphere, or produce fruits if there were neither light nor heat, as to regenerate men if I did not believe there were a Holy Ghost." (Henry Ward Beecher)
- Before the church can be sent into the world, it must be sent by the Spirit.
- "Cleanse the thoughts of our hearts by the inspiration of the Holy Spirit, that we may perfectly love thee, and worthily magnify thy Holy Name." (*Book of Common Prayers*)
- "But the Counselor, the Holy Spirit, whom the Father will send in my name, will teach you all things and will remind you of everything I have said to you." (John 14:26)
- "A man who is not following after holiness is following after hell." (Dr. P. F. Bresee)

- "... The Spirit helps us in our weaknesses. We do not know what we ought to pray for, but the Spirit himself intercedes for us with groans that words cannot express." (Romans 8:26)
- Who fills life afresh by directing both the heart and mind into doing what God loves? It is the breath of God's Spirit.
- Fan into flame the fire of holiness.
- The act of evangelism is the overflow of the Spirit in a person's heart.
- God does not want us to be unholy at any time.
- Only in the heart can a person be perfect.
- When the Holy Spirit comes, a hungering for excellence is the result.
- The true believer in the Holy Spirit is the person who sees the light from the lighthouse and avoids the rocks.
- The Holy Spirit speaks of a deeper life found to be richer, fuller, and spiritually satisfying to the Christian.
- Make holy living a holy habit.
- The Holy Spirit is like Tide® soap, the deeper the stain, the deeper the cleansing.
- Real leaders are ordinary people with extraordinary determination molded by the Spirit.
- We may not be able to direct the wind of the Spirit, but we can adjust the sails to catch the wind.
- Today's prepared spirit determines tomorrow's achievement in life.
- The difference between ordinary and extraordinary is the Holy Spirit.
- Holiness is practical living.
- "I am the Lord your God, consecrate yourselves and be holy, because I am holy." (Leviticus 11:44)
- "The power of the resurrection of Christ is the resident power of the Spirit. The Holy Ghost in man is God's dynamite in the soul." (Dr. P. F. Bresee)
- One of the jobs of the Holy Spirit is to prick the conscience of ethics and morals of people. Have you said, "Ouch," lately?
- Spiritual truth is conveyed with the Holy Spirit's help to anyone willing to listen.

- The Holy Spirit is our defense attorney.
- God's Spirit turns chickens into lions.
- Holiness begins in God.
- Holiness behavior conforms to the character of Christ.
- Our assurance, comfort, hope, and joy is in the complete holiness of the Father.
- God cannot help but act in a consistent manner with His holy character.
- Holiness is not like the light bulb — on again — off again.
- God hates sin because of His sinlessness.
- "Make every effort to live in peace with all men and to be holy; without holiness no one will see the Lord." (Hebrews 12:14)
- The Holy Spirit has come to make peace for us.
- Effective service to God is accomplished through a holiness lifestyle.
- Service to God cannot be offered in a dirty container.
- "The Holy Spirit makes us more aware of our lack of holiness to stimulate us to deeper yearning and striving for holiness." (Jerry Bridges)
- The world needs true examples of holiness.
- God does not force holiness on you ... He offers it to you free of charge.
- The heartbeat of holiness is the pulse of God.
- Being alive unto God comes through the indwelling of the Holy Spirit.
- The moral cesspools of life are removed by the whirlpools of the Spirit.
- Holiness removes the selfish sin.
- Holiness wipes away the moral and ethical evil that has accumulated in life.
- Holiness harmonizes us with the character of God.
- Holiness makes us morally fit for heaven.
- Holiness dwells on the almightiness of God.
- Holiness is like the engine that is fired up with a full head of steam and rolling towards heaven.
- Holiness is a bargain at any cost.
- Spirit-filled prayer is the best safeguard against backsliding.

- The Holy Spirit will fortify the soul for everyday spiritual battles.
- The standard by which we test God is how Holy He is.
- A holy person finds God at the center of the storm.
- "The Holy Spirit is the divine energy that produces the spiritual life." (Bertha Munro)
- The Spirit-filled Christian's theme is "ready to go, ready to stay, ready my place to fill."
- The Holy Spirit is the positive presence of Jesus.
- A Christian can be defined as someone who sets his goals, commits himself, then pursues his goals with the help of the Holy Spirit.
- The will to excel is through the Spirit from God.
- The Spirit, not chance, determines destiny.

www.ingramcontent.com/pod-product-compliance
Lightning Source LLC
Chambersburg PA
CBHW071748040426
42446CB00012B/2494